·TATTOO·
INSPIRATION
·COMPENDIUM·
AN IMAGE ARCHIVE FOR TATTOO ARTISTS and DESIGNERS

UNITED WE STAND · DIVIDED WE FALL·

E PLURIBUS UNUM.

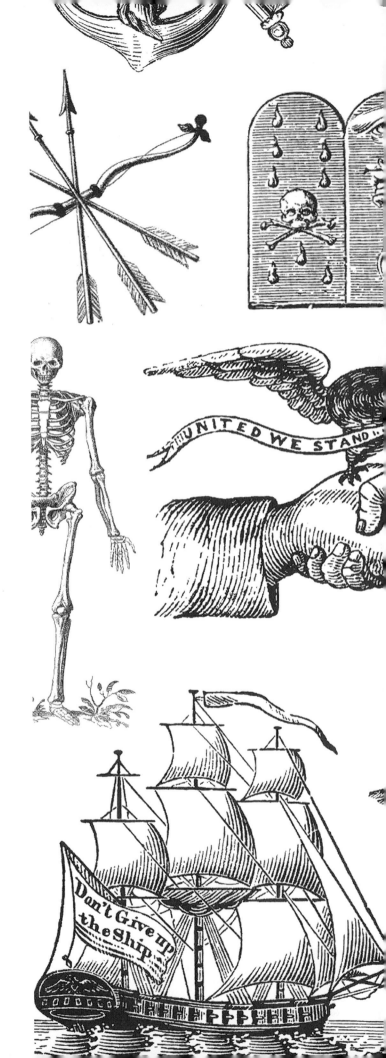

INTRODUCTION

In the intricate world of tattoo artistry, where each inked stroke carries a narrative and every design is a canvas for personal expression, lies a boundless realm of creativity waiting to be explored. Welcome to "The Tattoo Inspiration Compendium" – a mesmerising voyage through an anthology of visual wonders curated exclusively for tattoo artists and designers. Within these pages, the essence of human emotion, culture, and symbolism converge, offering an eclectic array of imagery to ignite the imagination and redefine the boundaries of tattoo design.

As the inked tapestry of the modern world continues to evolve, so do the tastes and aspirations of artists and those who seek their skilled hands. This compendium is not just a collection of static visuals; it's a dynamic source of inspiration that bridges the gap between the traditional and the contemporary, the culturally rooted and the boldly innovative. From the rich heritage of ancient iconography to the avant-garde fusion of styles, every page turn reveals a new facet of inspiration.

Whether you're an aspiring tattoo artist seeking fresh avenues of inspiration or a seasoned artist looking to revitalise your creative reservoir, "The Tattoo Inspiration Compendium" promises a symphony of visual marvels to spark your imagination. It beckons you to transcend the conventional and venture into uncharted territories of artistry, where the skin becomes a canvas and stories are etched in ink.

TABLE OF CONTENTS

DOWNLOAD YOUR FILES

Downloading your files is simple. To access your digital files, please go to the last page of this book and follow the instructions.

For technical assistance, please email:
info@vaulteditions.com

Bibliographical Note

This book is a new work created by Vault Editions Ltd.

ISBN: 978-1925968422

VAULT EDITIONS

TATTOO INSPIRATION COMPENDIUM

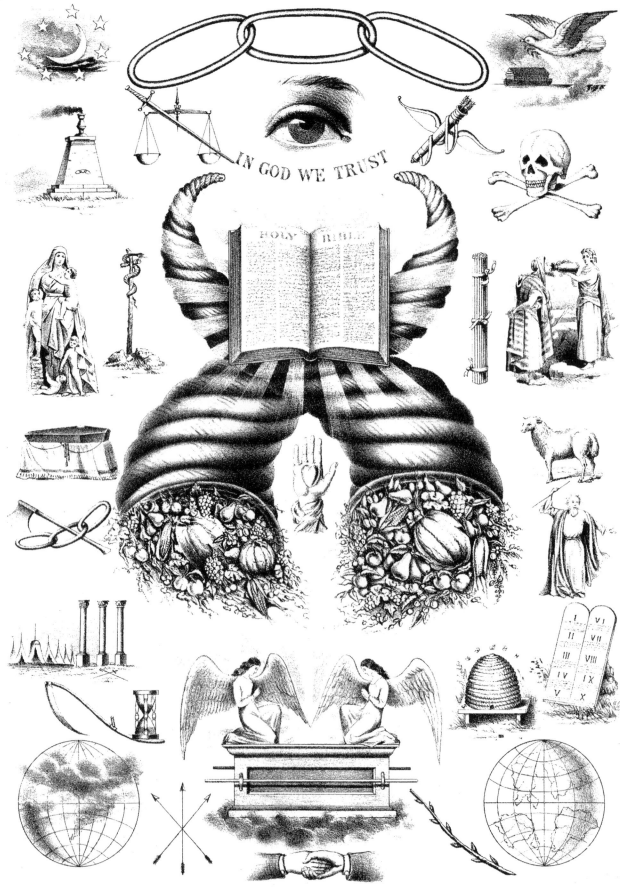

02

03

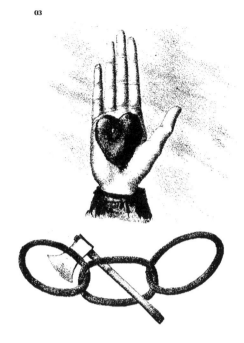

04

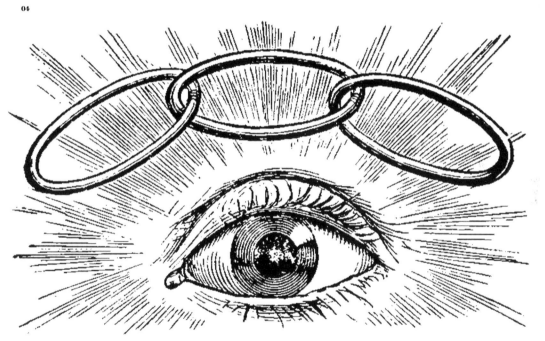

05

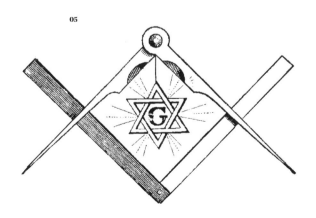

06

07

08

09

10

TATTOO INSPIRATION COMPENDIUM

11

12

13

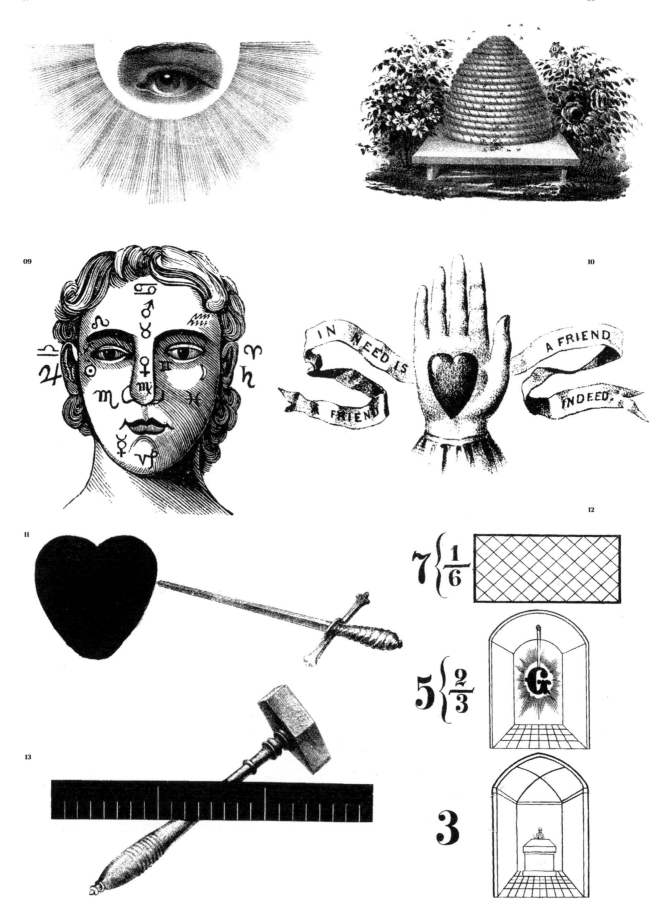

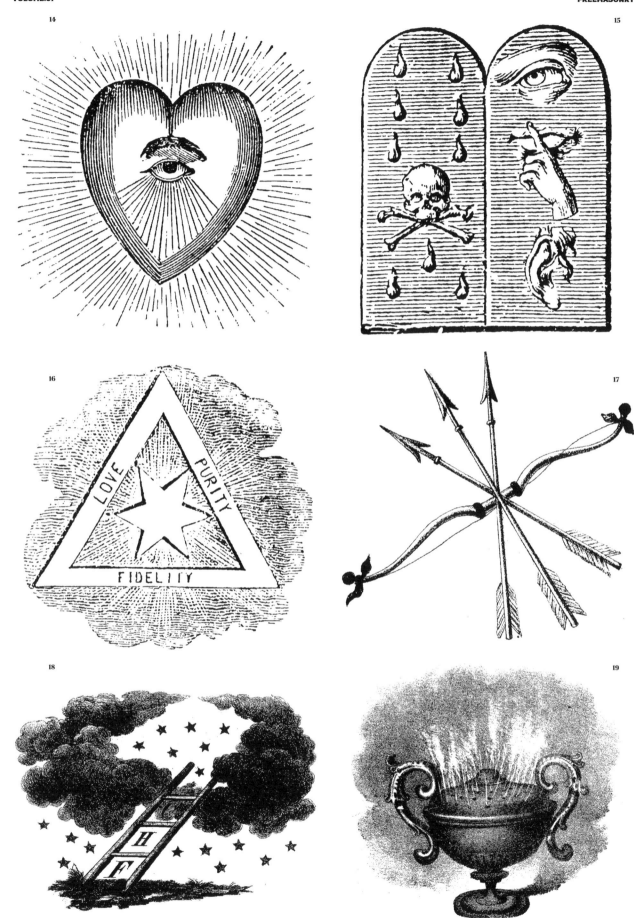

14

15

16

17

18

19

TATTOO INSPIRATION COMPENDIUM

LOVE

PURITY

FIDELITY

20

21

22

TATTOO INSPIRATION COMPENDIUM

23

24

25

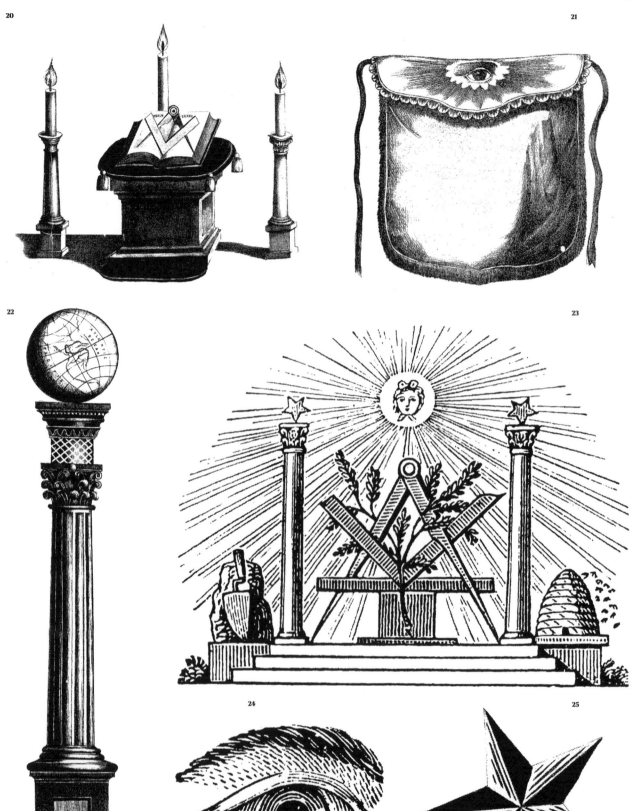

26

27

28

29

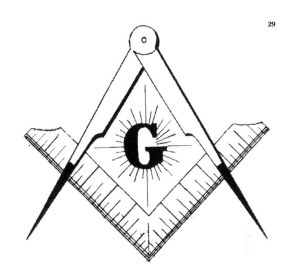

30

31

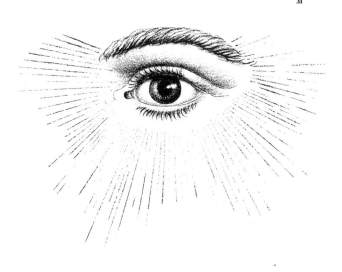

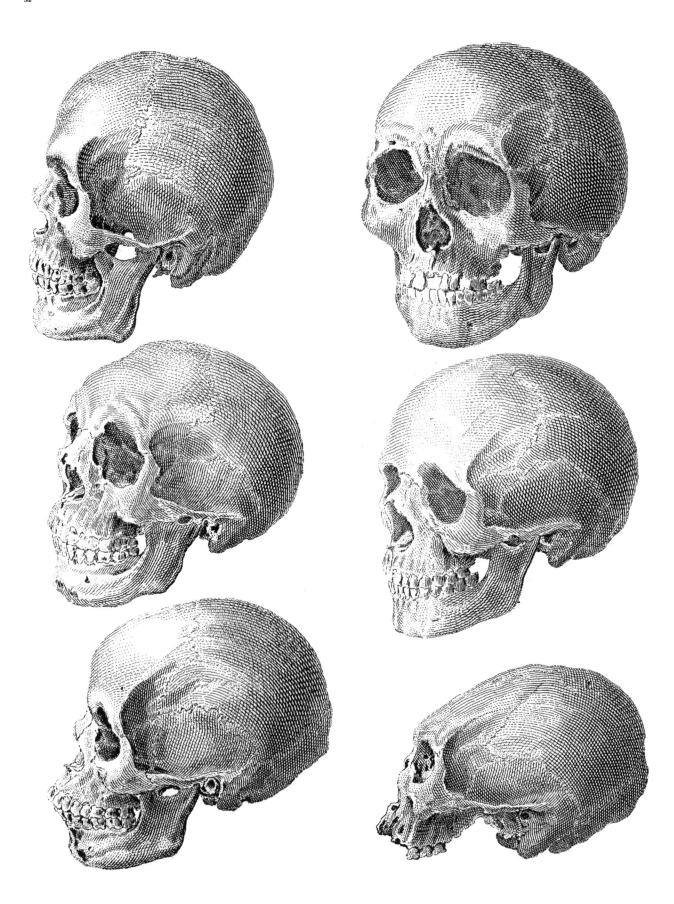

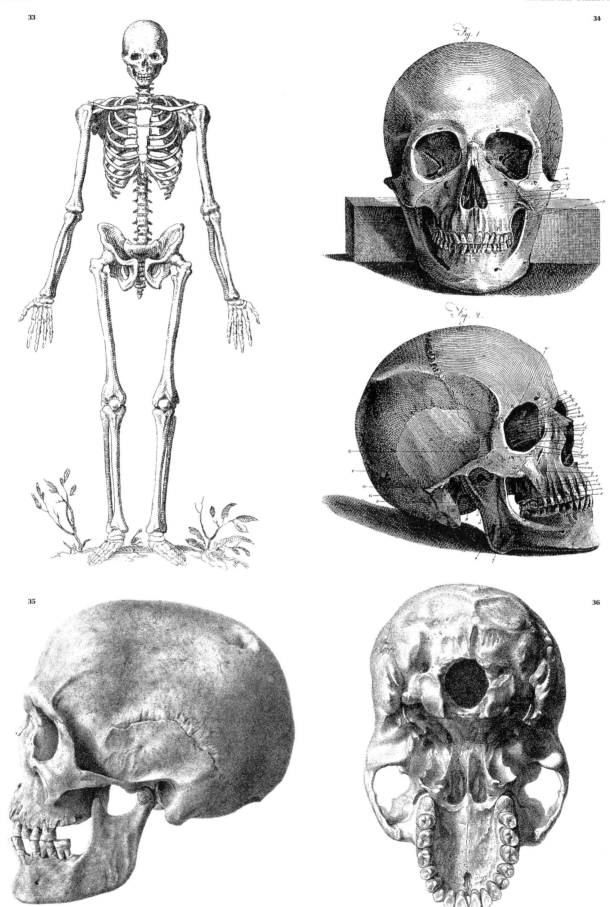

TATTOO INSPIRATION COMPENDIUM

37

TATTOO INSPIRATION COMPENDIUM

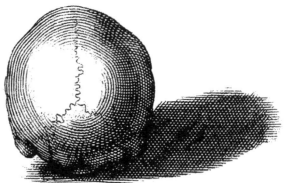

38

39

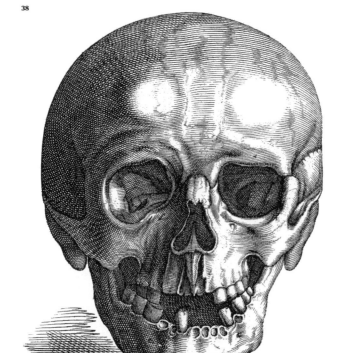

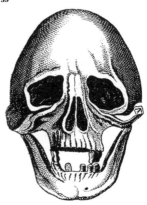

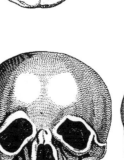

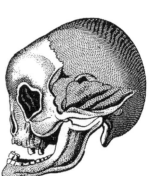

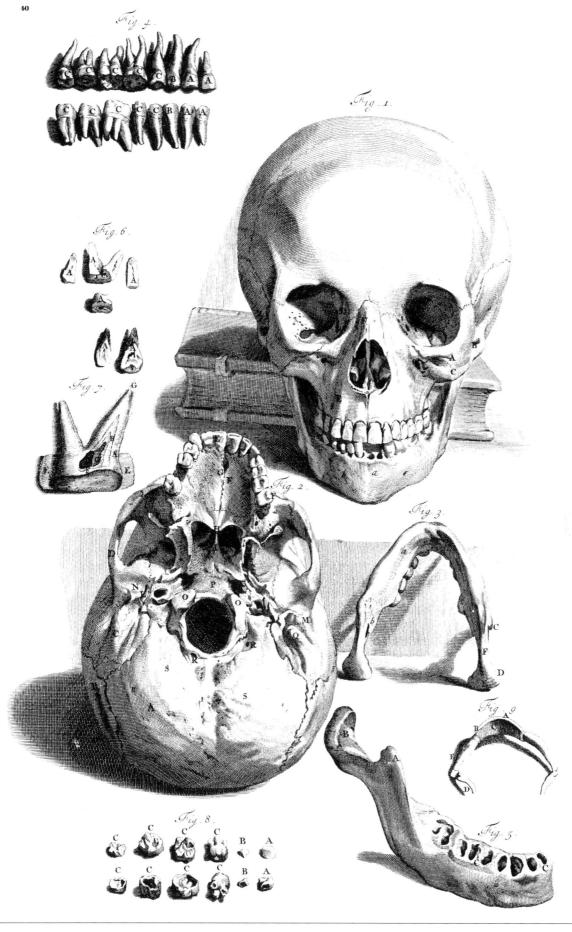

Fig. 4.

Fig. 1.

Fig. 6.

Fig. 7.

Fig. 2.

Fig. 3.

Fig. 9.

Fig. 5.

Fig. 8.

TATTOO INSPIRATION COMPENDIUM

TATTOO INSPIRATION COMPENDIUM

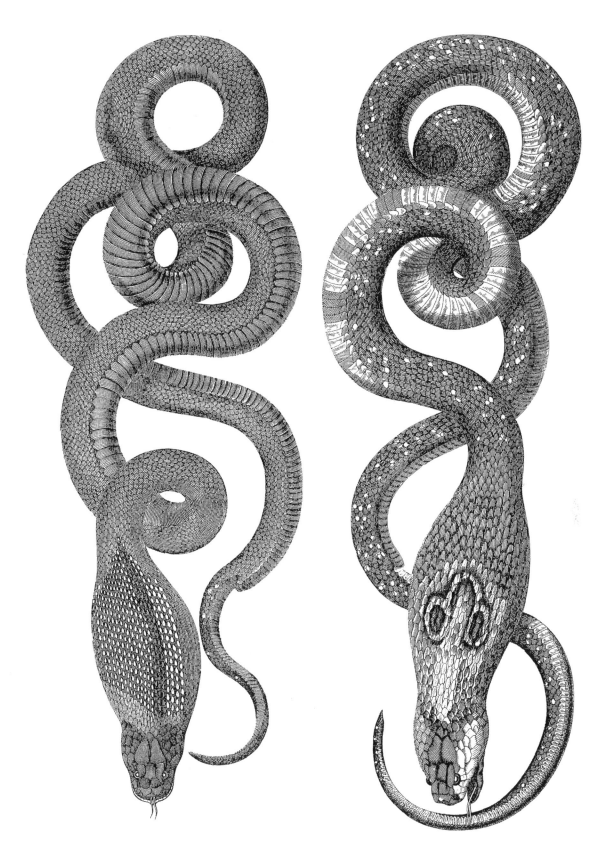

TATTOO INSPIRATION COMPENDIUM

TATTOO INSPIRATION COMPENDIUM

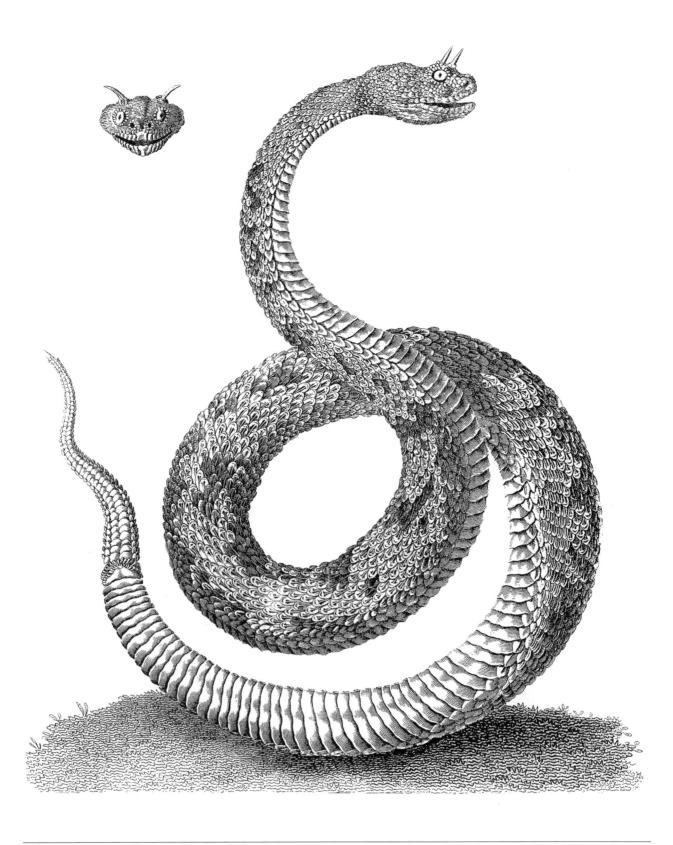

47

TATTOO INSPIRATION COMPENDIUM

50

TATTOO INSPIRATION COMPENDIUM

TATTOO INSPIRATION COMPENDIUM

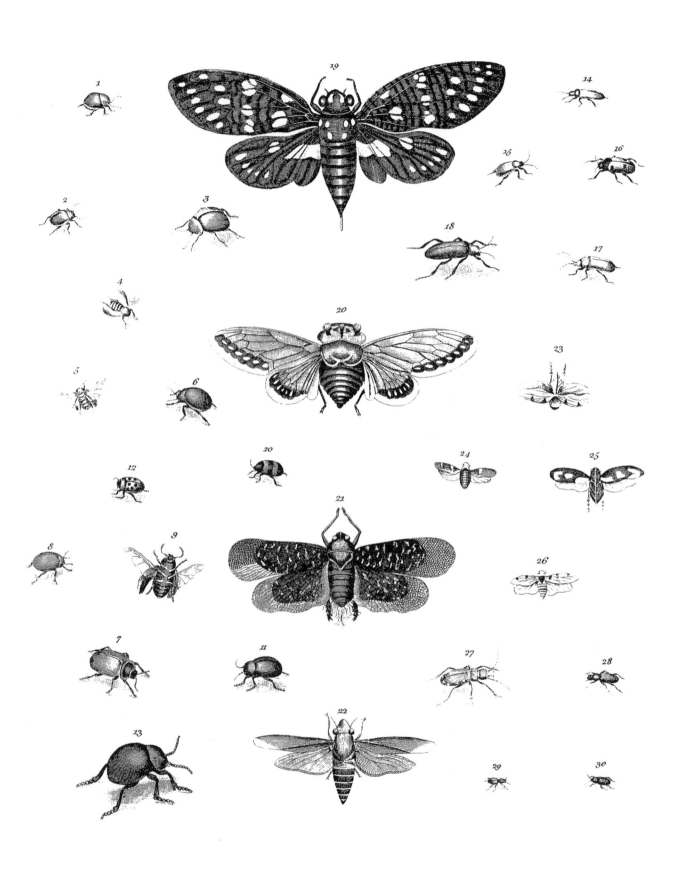

54

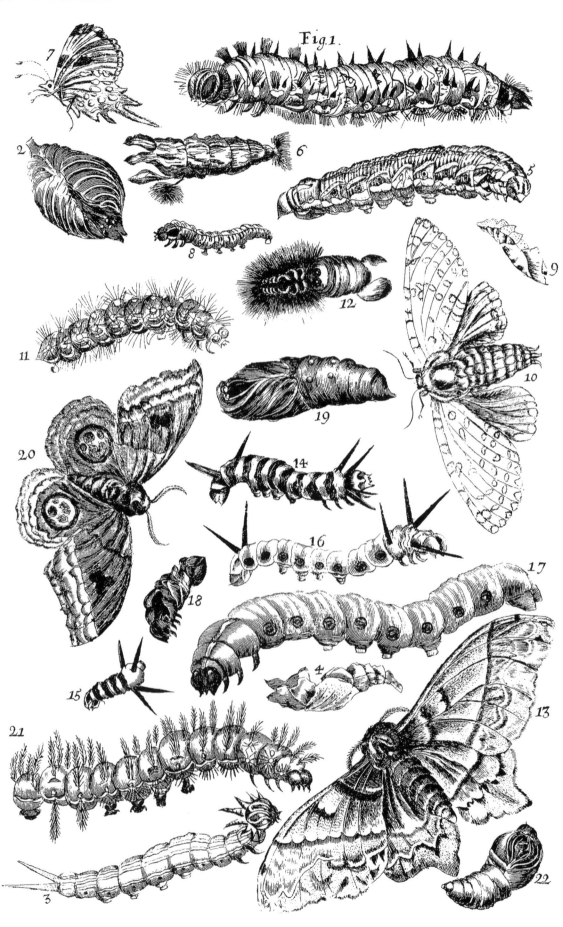

Fig.1.

55

TATTOO INSPIRATION COMPENDIUM

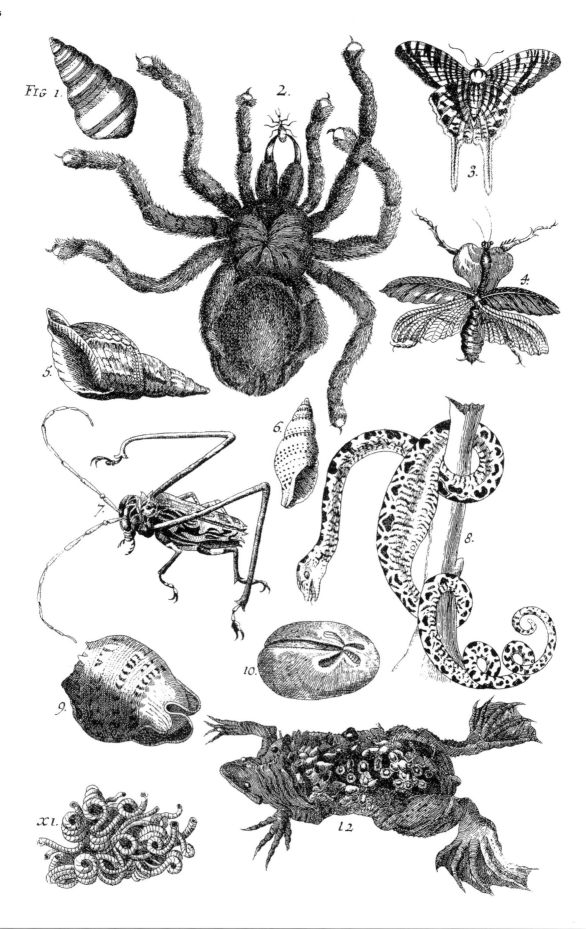

57

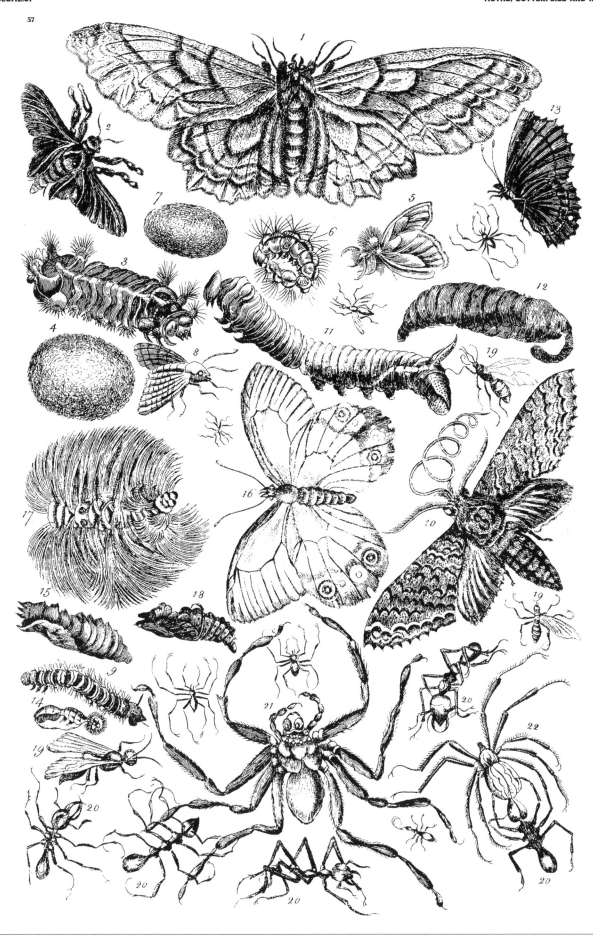

TATTOO INSPIRATION COMPENDIUM

58

p

o

q

f

y

v

6

59

60

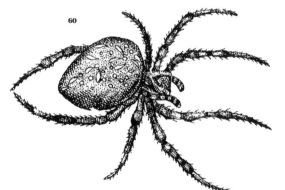

61

TATTOO INSPIRATION COMPENDIUM

TATTOO INSPIRATION COMPENDIUM

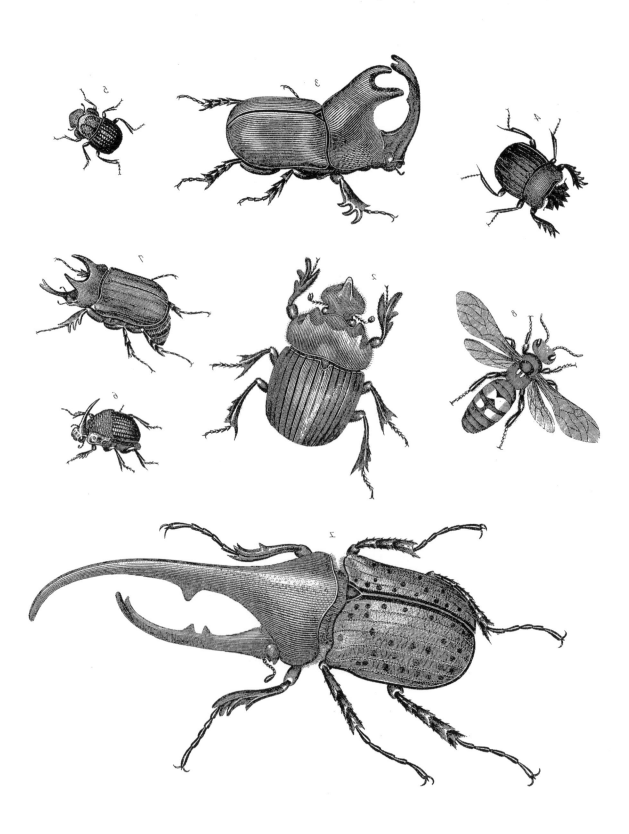

64

65

66

67

68

69

70

71

72

73

74

75

76

When Freedom, from her mountain height,
      Unfurled her Standard to the air,
She tore the azure robes of light,
      And set the stars of glory there !
Then from his mansion in the sun,
      She called her EAGLE bearer down,
And gave into his mighty hand,
      The Symbol of her chosen land !

82

83

84

85

86

87

88

89

90

LIBERTY AND UNION.

91

92

93

94

95

96

97

98

99

100

101

102

103

104

105

106

107

108

109

110

111

112

113

114

115

TATTOO INSPIRATION COMPENDIUM

116

117

118

119

120

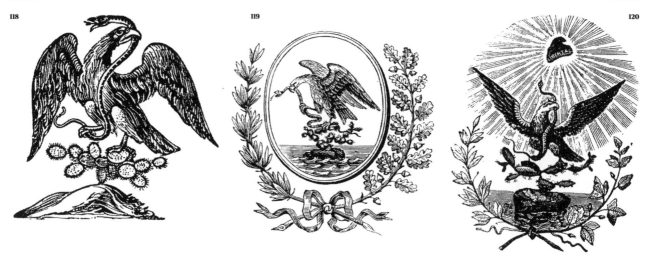

121

122

123

124

125

126

127

128

129

130

131

132

133

134

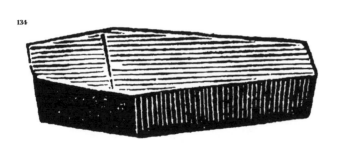

135

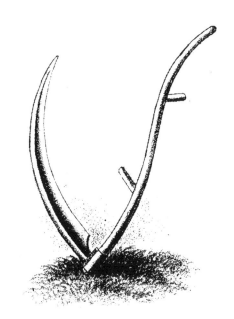

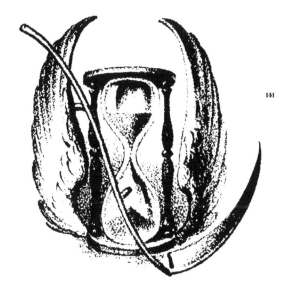

145

144

DUST THOU ART,

TO DUST SHALT THOU RETURN.

146

147

148

FOREVER AMEN. AND EVER

150

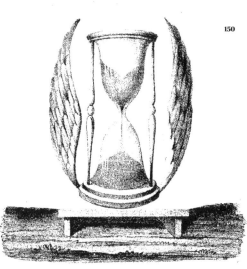

151

TATTOO INSPIRATION COMPENDIUM

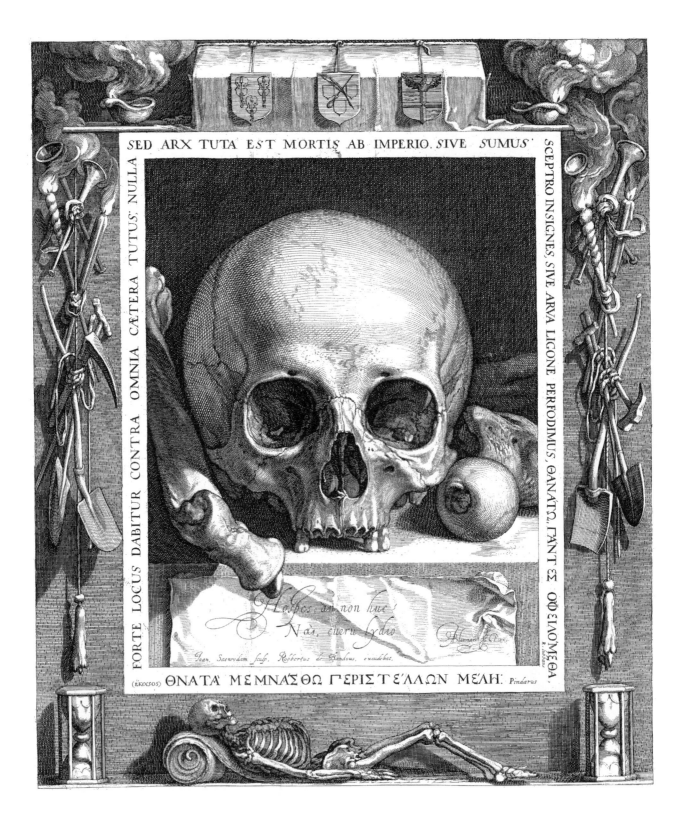

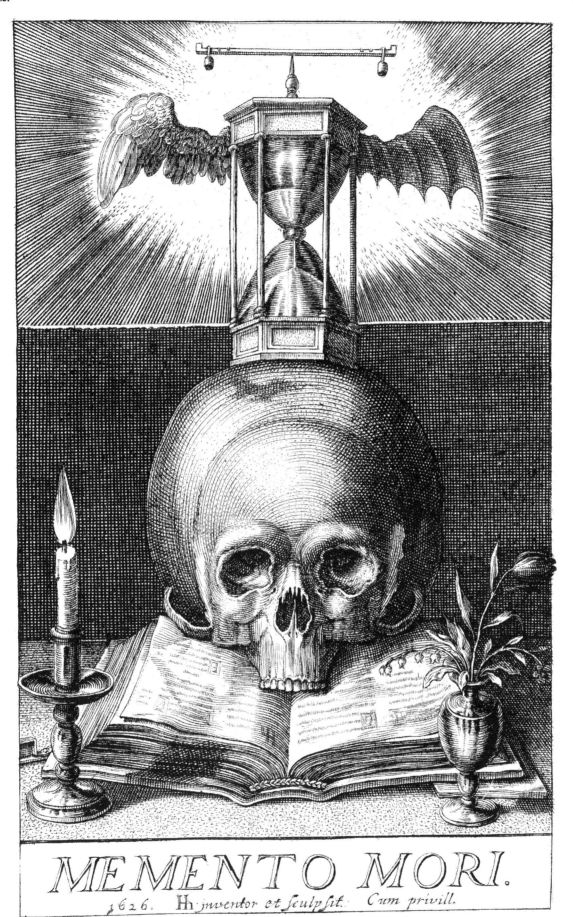

MEMENTO MORI.

1626. H: inventor et sculpsit. Cum privill.

154

155

TATTOO INSPIRATION COMPENDIUM

156

157

158

159

TATTOO INSPIRATION COMPENDIUM

160

TATTOO INSPIRATION COMPENDIUM

161

162

163

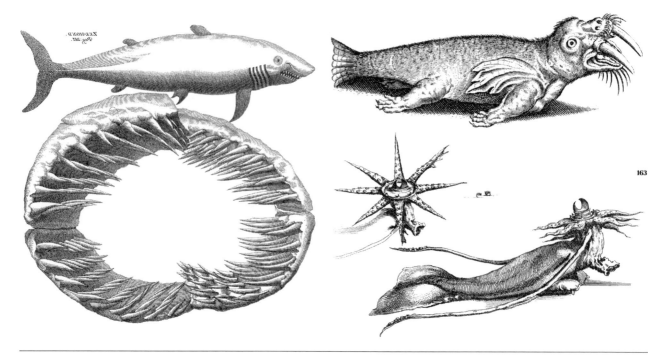

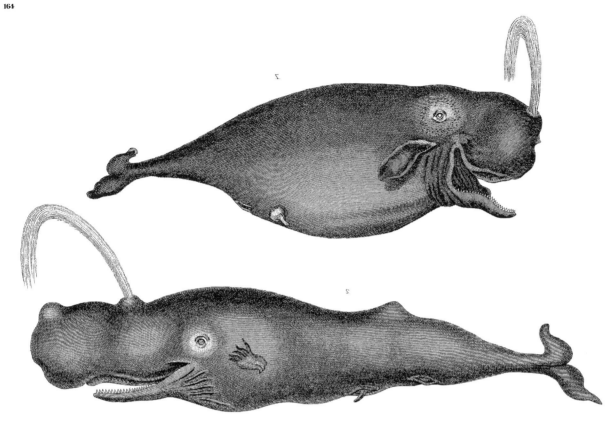

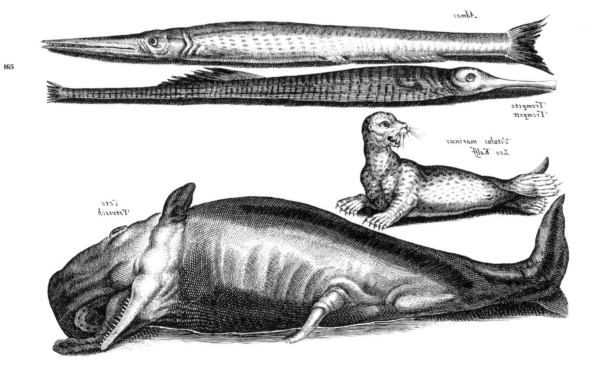

166

167

MERMAID.

TATTOO INSPIRATION COMPENDIUM

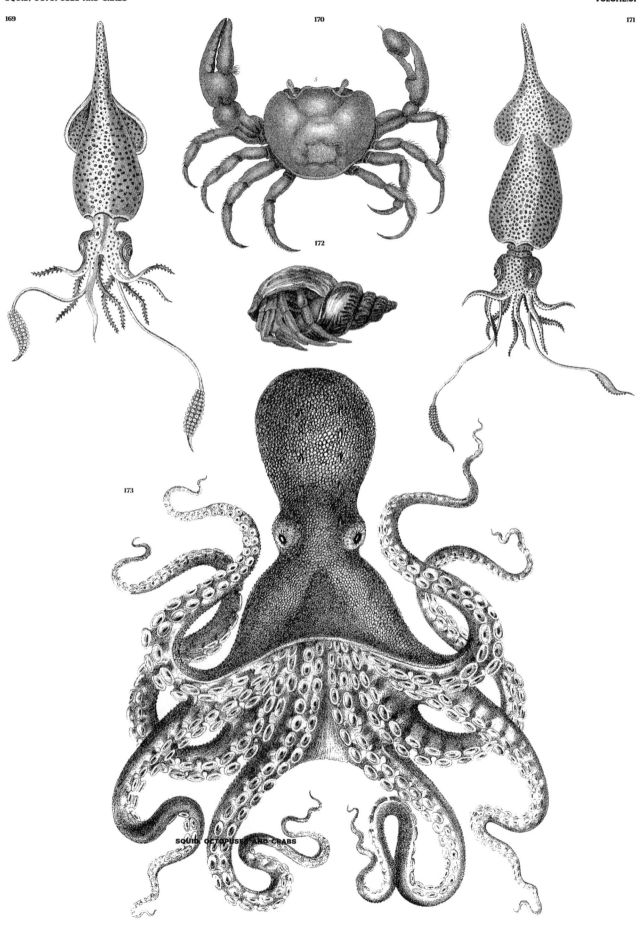

174

177

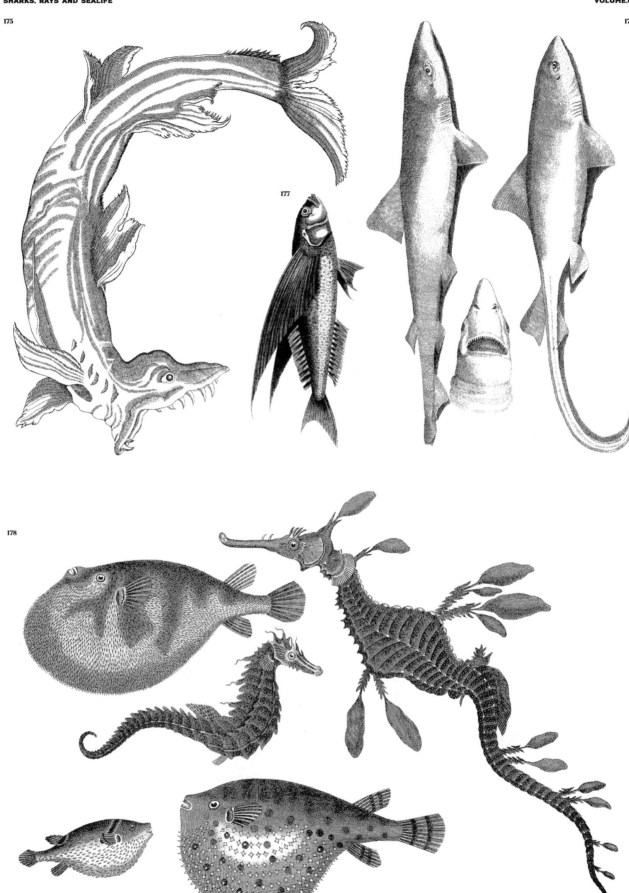

178

179

180

181

182

183

184

187

188

189

190

191

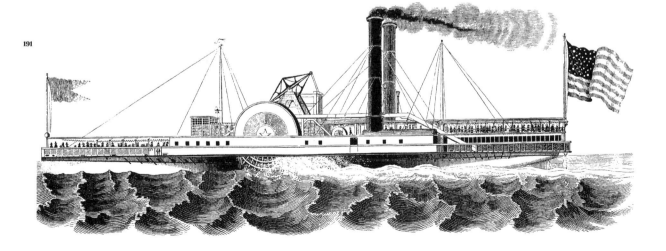

193

194

195

196

197

198

199

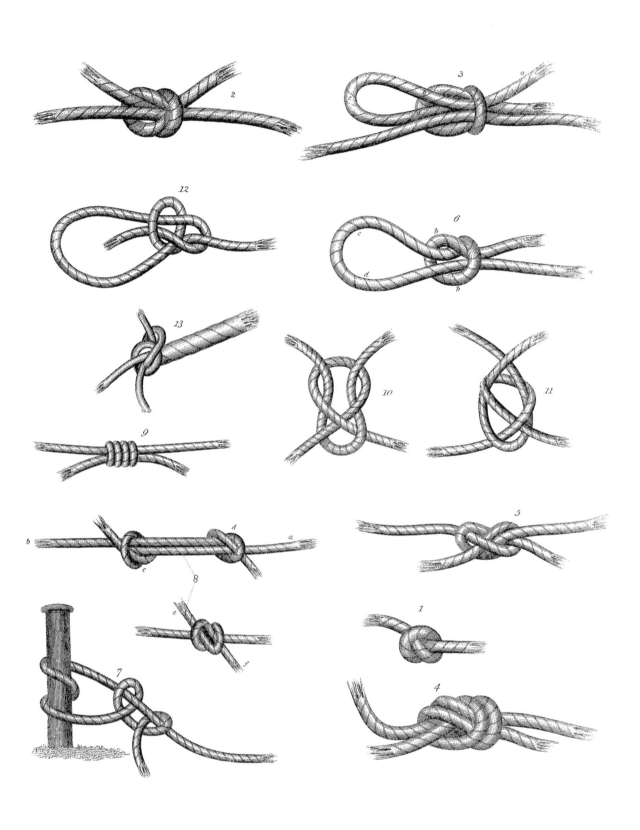

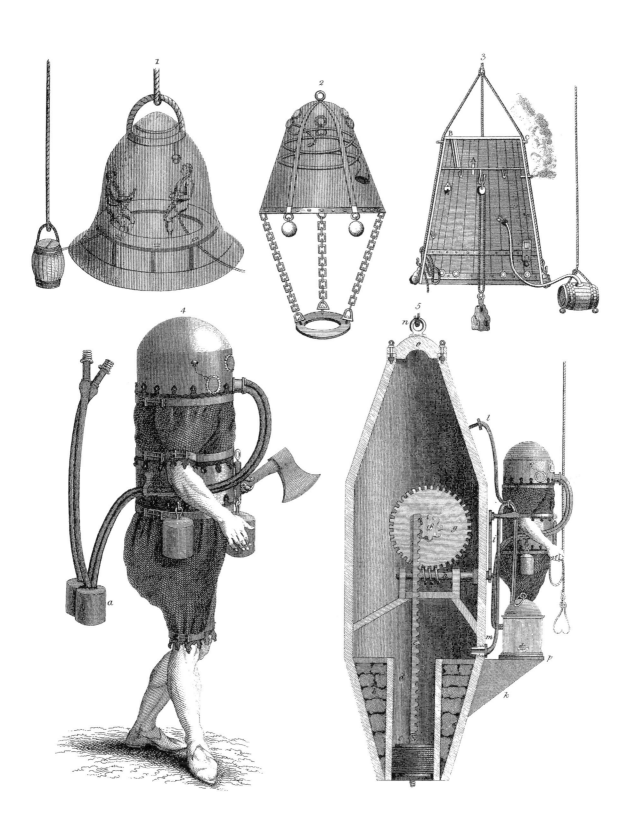

TATTOO INSPIRATION COMPENDIUM

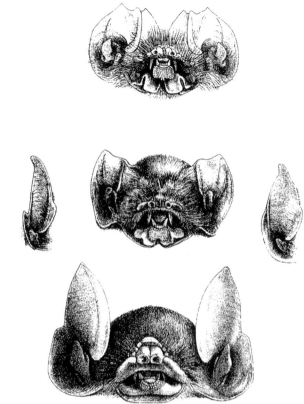

204

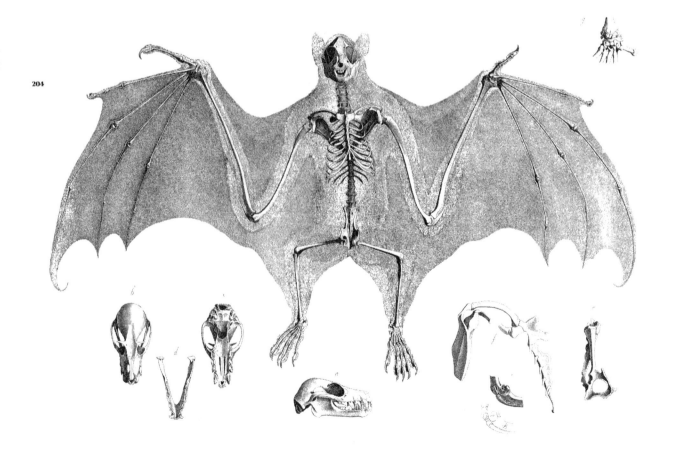

206

207

208

209

210

TATTOO INSPIRATION COMPENDIUM

Wat baet keers off bril, als den WL niet sien en wil.

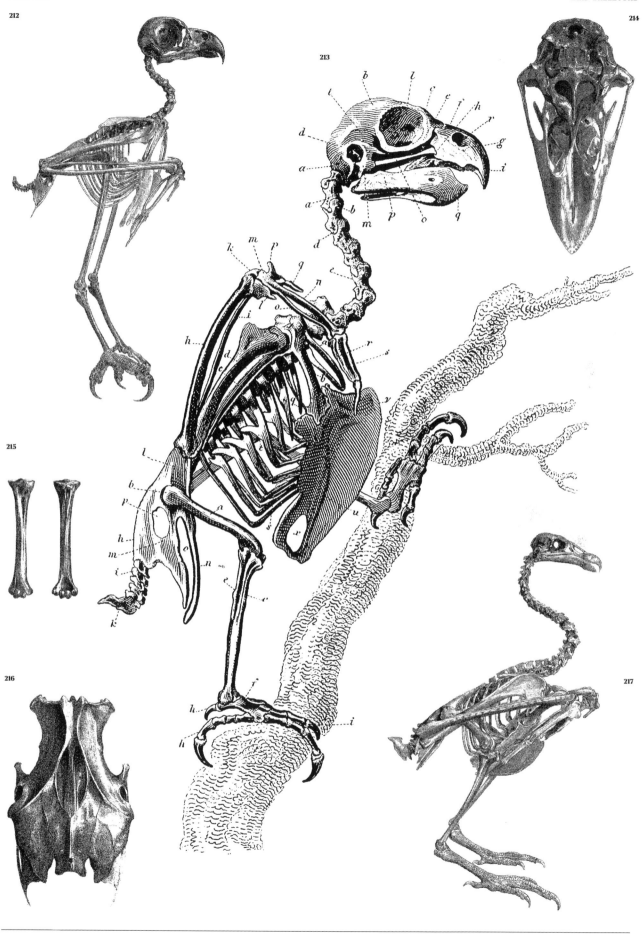

219

220

221

222

223

224

225

226

227

235

236

237

238

239

240

242

241

243

244

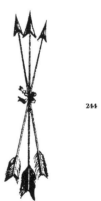

245

246

247

248

ASPICIENTES IN AVCTOREM FIDEI, ET CONSVMMATOREM IESVM. *ad Hebr.* XII

P P. *Rubens pinxit.*   P. *Dannoot fecit.*

249

250

251

252

S. PHILIPPVS

253

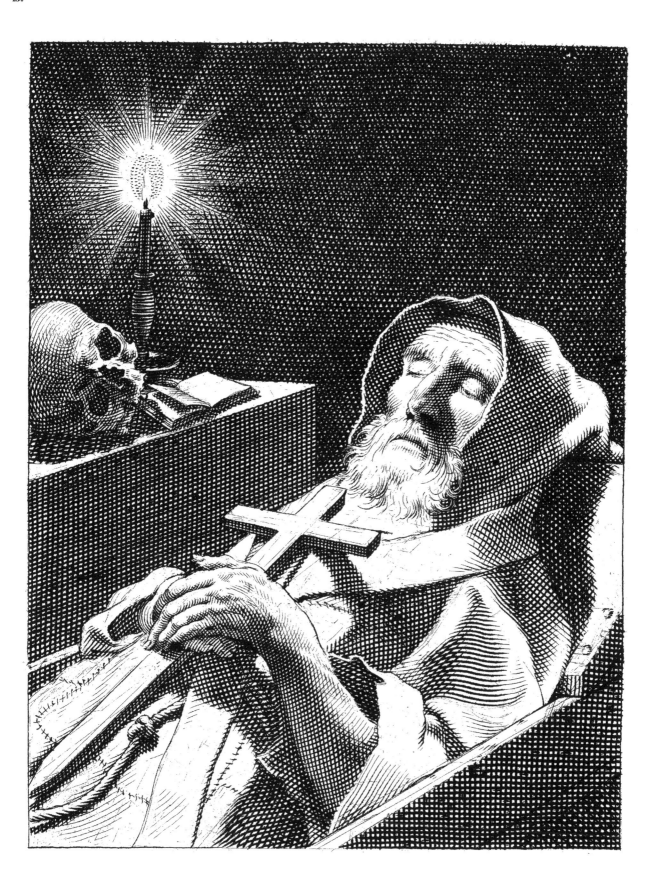

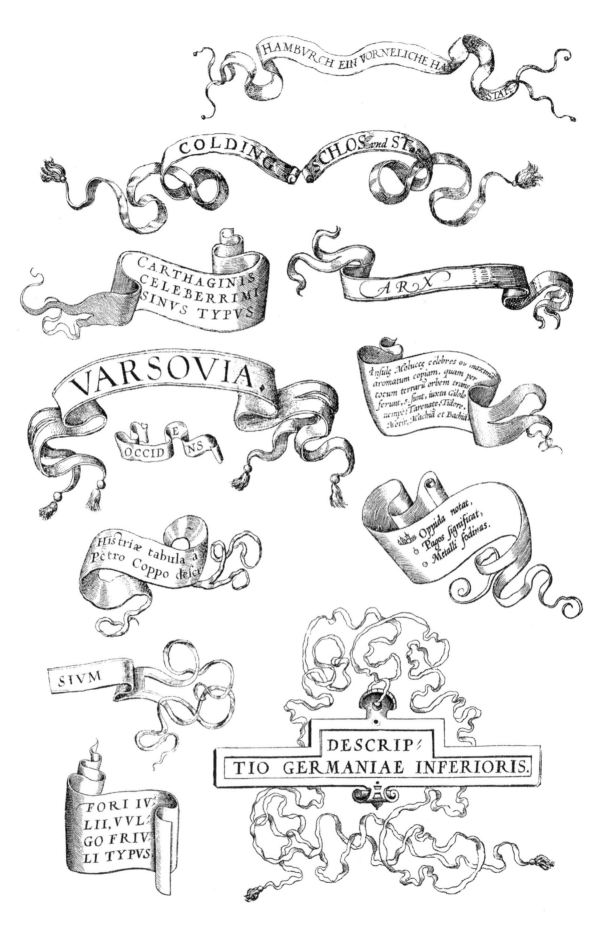

257

TATTOO INSPIRATION COMPENDIUM

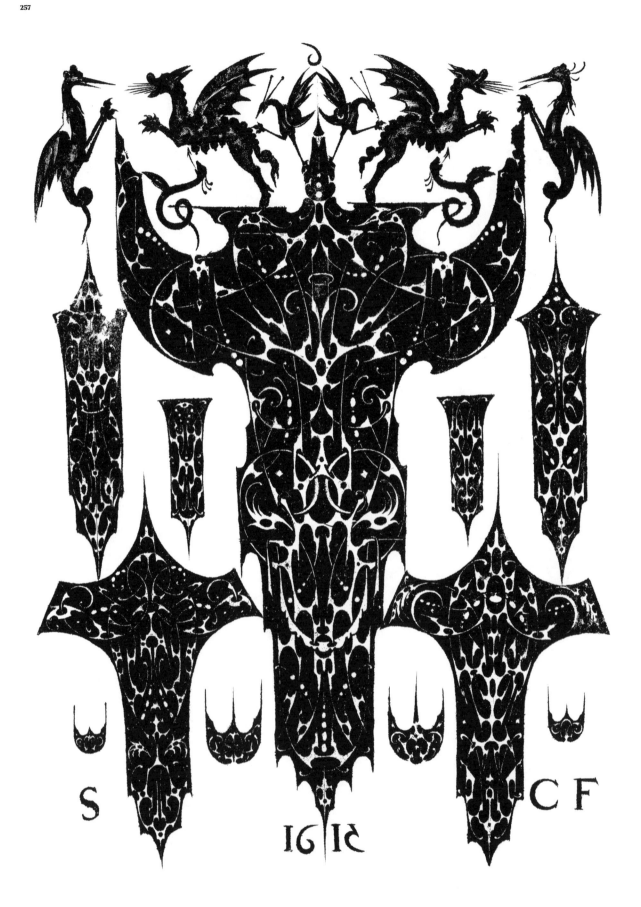

TATTOO INSPIRATION COMPENDIUM

259

TATTOO INSPIRATION COMPENDIUM

261

Bedford

Devonshire

Marlborough

Rutland

Brandon

Ancaster

Portland

Manchester

Dorset

Newcastle

Northumberland

266

TATTOO INSPIRATION COMPENDIUM

STO CADO FIDE ET ARMIS

AQUILA NON CAPTAT MUSCAS

QUO VIRTUS VOCAT

267

SOIT · QUI · MAL · Y · PENSE

HONI

ET · MON

DIEU

DROIT

273

274

TATTOO INSPIRATION COMPENDIUM

275

276

277

278

279

280

281

TATTOO INSPIRATION COMPENDIUM

282   283   284

285   287

286

288   289

TATTOO INSPIRATION COMPENDIUM

290   291   292

293   295

294

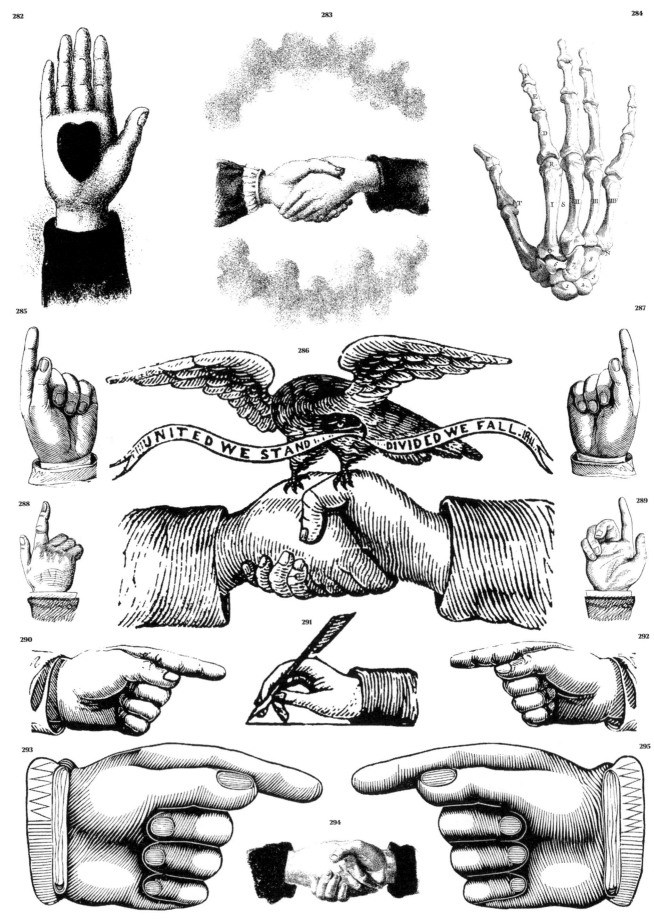

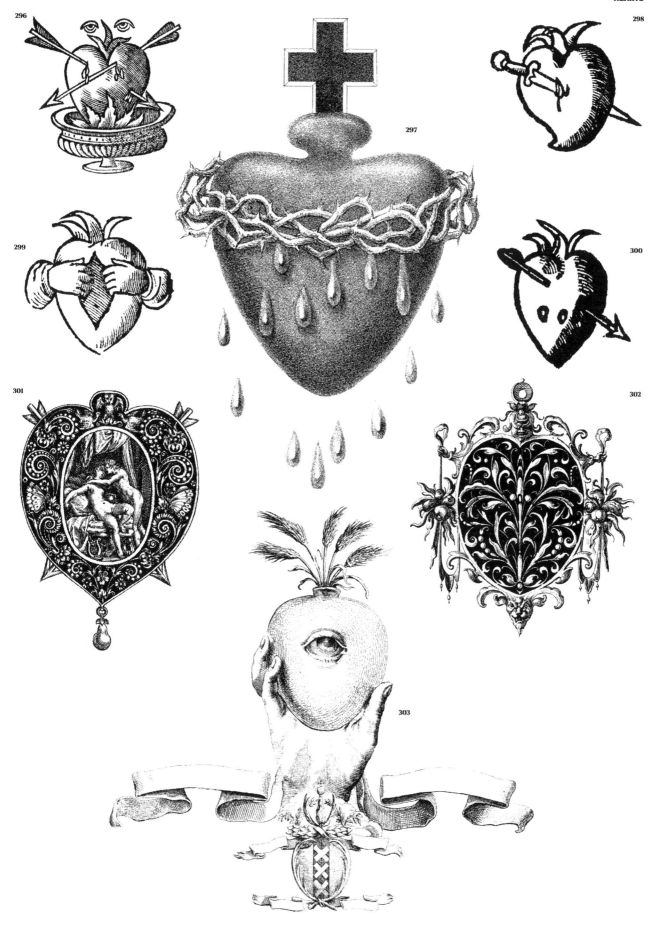

TATTOO INSPIRATION COMPENDIUM

TATTOO INSPIRATION COMPENDIUM

304

305

306

309

308

307

310

311

312

TATTOO INSPIRATION COMPENDIUM

313

314

315

316

317

319

318

320

TATTOO INSPIRATION COMPENDIUM

321   322   323   324

325

326

327

328

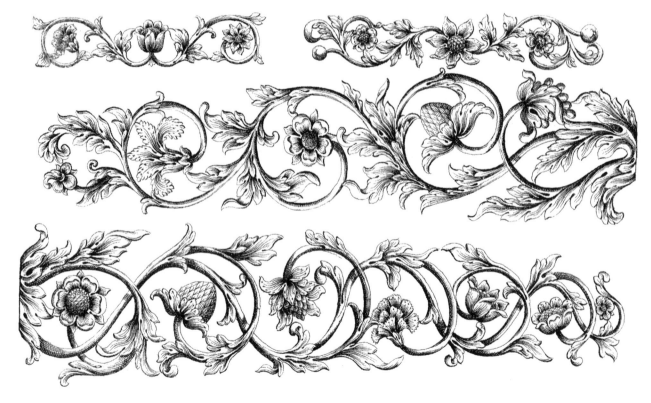

329

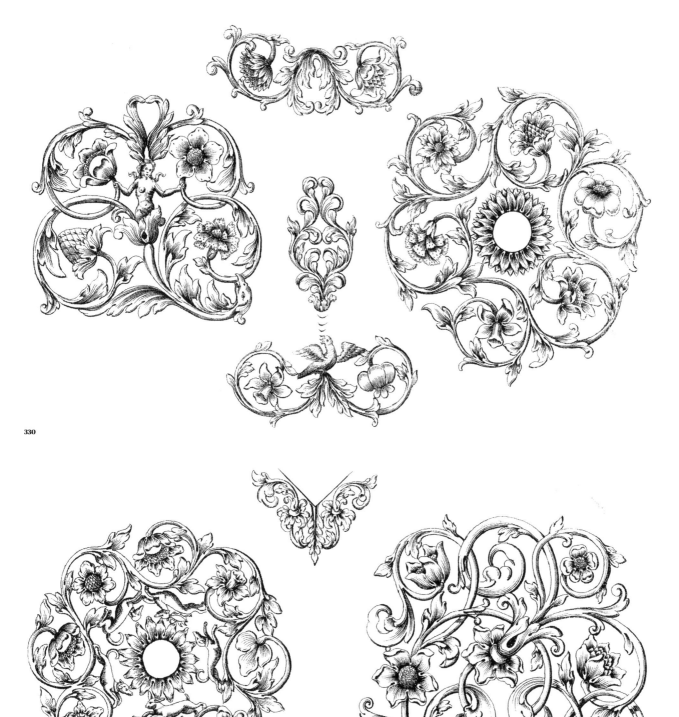

330

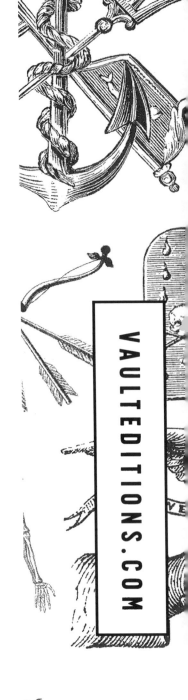

LEARN MORE

At Vault Editions, our mission is to create the world's most diverse and comprehensive collection of image archives available for artists, designers and curious minds. If you have enjoyed this book, you can find more of our titles available at vaulteditions.com.

REVIEW THIS BOOK

As a small, family-owned independent publisher, reviews help spread the word about our work. We would be incredibly grateful if you could leave an honest review of this title wherever you purchased this book.

JOIN OUR COMMUNITY

Are you a creative and curious individual? If so, you will love our community on Instagram. Every day we share bizarre and beautiful artwork ranging from 17th and 18th-century natural history and scientific illustration, to mythical beasts, ornamental designs, anatomical illustration and more. Join our community of 100K+ people today—search @vault_editions on Instagram.

DOWNLOAD YOUR FILES

STEP ONE

Enter the following web address in your web browser on a desktop computer.

www.vaulteditions.com/pages/tic

STEP TWO

Enter the following unique password to access the download page.

tac2734rgd5

STEP THREE

Follow the prompts to access your high-resolution files.

TECHNICAL ASSISTANCE

For all technical assistance, please email: info@vaulteditions.com

Made in the USA
Las Vegas, NV
27 October 2023

79808441R00065